The Many ~~Tails~~ Tales of Mitzie the Mouse

The Many ~~Tails~~ Tales of Mitzie the Mouse

By Irma Crutchfield

Illustrated by Julia Leal and John Lavery

Copyright © 2017 by Irma Crutchfield

All rights reserved. Except for brief excerpts for review purposes, no part of this book may be used or reproduced in any form without the written permission of the publisher.

Crutchfield, Irma
Summary: Mrs. Gracie teaches her new mouse friend, Mitzie, how to know Jesus and praise Him. Mitzie shares Jesus with her new friend, Rainey.

Illustrators: John Lavery and Julia Leal
First Edition
A Children's book

ISBN:
Hardcover: 978-1-941516-32-4
Paperback: 978-1-941516-22-5

Published by Franklin Scribes Publishers.
Franklin Scribes is a registered trademark of Franklin Scribes Publishers.
franklinscribeswrites@gmail.com
www.franklinscribes.com
Contact the author at www.franklinscribes/irma-crutchfield/

Front and back book covers by Thompson Printing Solutions
This book was printed in the United States of America.

Acknowledgment

First, I want to give thanks to my Lord and Savior for giving me the dream of a little mouse and Mrs. Gracie.

Thanks to my husband, Monty, for helping me convert my thoughts into words and for his love and patience. Thanks to my children, Tony, Jennifer and James for their support and love. I thank my grandchildren, Kailey and Benjamin, for having patience with me during the many hours I worked on these stories.

To the Christian Writers Group of San Antonio: This book would not have been completed without them. Thanks to my friends, Judy Watters and Sandra Cleary of Franklin Scribes, for walking me through the editing and publishing of Mitzie. And many thanks to my illustrators, Julia Leal and John Lavery, who brought Mitzie to life. Many thanks to all.

Mitzie Mouse

Mrs. Gracie Meets Mitzie

Mrs. Gracie went outside to check on her garden. She looked at her strawberries first. Then she checked her squash, peas, and carrots.

"Jesus is good," Mrs. Gracie said to herself. She looked up to the sky. "Thank you, Jesus, for the two days of rain. Look at my garden grow. You have made it beautiful."

Mrs. Gracie turned to go back to her house. She saw something move in one of her dirt-filled flowerpots. A baby mouse lay curled up with its tiny tail wrapped around its body. She picked up the wet, frail baby mouse and cupped it in the palm of her warm hand.

"You look very cold, little one," she said as she looked into the mouse's tired eyes. "Why don't you take a ride in my warm apron pocket and come inside with me?"

She carried the cold little mouse into the warm kitchen and placed the baby mouse in her basket she used to bring fruit from the garden. She covered the basket with a warm dishtowel and set it next to her rocking chair near the fireplace.

"This will keep you warm," Mrs. Gracie said, "and I can watch over you while I read my Bible." Mrs. Gracie wondered what she should read to the little mouse. "I know," she said, "I will read to my new friend about how Jesus loves all the little children."

Mrs. Gracie picked up her Bible and sat in her rocking chair. "Listen, little one. In the book of Matthew, Jesus said, 'Let the little children come to me, and do not hinder them, for the kingdom of heaven belongs to such as these.'" She looked down at the little mouse all curled up. "I will keep watch over you all night." And she did just that.

In the morning, the mouse was very hungry. Mrs. Gracie put tiny bits of cheese and bread on a small saucer. She also filled a bottle cap with milk. Her movements were slow and loving. The little mouse feared nothing at all, as she ate and drank until everything was gone.

Mrs. Gracie smiled. She picked the little mouse out of the basket, wrapped it gently in her apron on her lap, and started to rock back and forth in her rocking chair. When the mouse fell asleep, Mrs. Gracie whispered to her. "I will teach you to read so you can learn the Good News. I will teach you all about Jesus and the Ten Commandments. You will learn right from wrong." She picked up her Bible and read the Ten Commandments." That's a lot to learn right now," she said. "I will teach you one at a time. For now, you need a name."

Mrs. Gracie looked at the baby mouse and tried to think of a name. She could not think of one she liked, so she turned on the television to watch an old movie. There was a sweet little girl in the movie named Mitzie

"That's perfect," she told the mouse. "Your name will be Mitzie." She put Mitzie and her basket in an old birdcage that she used when she raised finches. "I have two cats," Mrs. Gracie told Mitzie, "but until you become friends, this birdcage will keep you safe."

Mrs. Gracie was happy that Jesus had brought her a new friend. She would do her very best to teach Mitzie the love of Jesus.

Start children off on the way they should go,
and even when they are old,
they will not turn from it.

Proverbs 22:6 (NIV)

Mrs. Gracie's Garden

Ten Commandments

Every day Mrs. Gracie gave Mitzie little pieces of cheese, bread, fruit, and a bottle cap full of milk. Soon Mitzie was running around and playing in the cage. Since the sun was out and the ground was dry, Mrs. Gracie brought an old birdhouse from outdoors into the kitchen and put it on the table.

"I will paint the birdhouse a pretty yellow," said Mrs. Gracie, "and hang it high enough in the old pecan tree, so it won't get flooded when it rains." She put Mitzie in the little house with a small matchbox filled with slices of fruit.

Mitzie loved her new home. There was so much to see from the front porch of her birdhouse. "I will plant a garden of strawberries and peas just for you," Mrs. Gracie said, "exactly where I first found you."

Mitzie watched Mrs. Gracie day after day as she watered her plants and pulled weeds that grew close to the good plants. Soon the strawberries and peas started to sprout and bloom. Mitzie was excited. Every day she checked to see if they were ready to eat. One day the strawberries were ready to pick. She giggled and spun around in tiny circles!

Mitzie tried to pull one off the vine. She pulled and pulled, but the vine was too strong for a little mouse.

"Mitzie," said Mrs. Gracie, "what's wrong, little one?"

A tear rolled down Mitzie's cheek.

"Look, Mitzie," Mrs. Gracie said. "Just twist it off the stem." She picked the biggest strawberry and put it in the birdhouse for Mitzie. She also put a small piece of paper close by.

Mitzie took a big bite of the strawberry. She ate and ate until her stomach couldn't hold any more. After eating, she got very sleepy. She washed her hands, her face and whiskers and brushed her teeth. Before she went to sleep, she unrolled the paper that Mrs. Gracie had put in her house. On the top of the paper were three words in big letters: THE TEN COMMANDMENTS. She decided to learn them so that she could be like Mrs. Gracie.

After Mitzie read all Ten Commandments, she got on her knees next to her tiny bed, folded her little paws, and prayed, "Thank you, Jesus, for Mrs. Gracie. Keep Mrs. Gracie safe and most of all, thank you for being Jesus. Good night, Jesus. Oh, and thank you for the green peas, sweet strawberries, and my new home. Amen

The Ten Commandments

You shall not have any gods before me.
You shall not have idols.
You shall not use God's name in vain.
Remember the Sabbath and keep it Holy.
Honor your parents.
You shall not murder.
You shall not commit adultery.
You shall not steal.
You shall not lie.
You shall not covet.

Exodus 20:1 – 17 (NIV)

Mitzie Meets Bullfrog

WEBS, BUGS AND SPIDERS! OH, MY!

Mitzie sat by the pond and watched the clouds change shapes from a cat to a dove to a lamb. The frogs, spiders, and crickets that lived in the backyard were all Mitzie's friends. But she wanted a friend like herself. She would go under the fence and past the backyard. Before she went, she prayed for Jesus to protect her. Mrs. Gracie had read Psalm 23 from the Bible one time when Mitzie was afraid of a storm. "I will read that now," Mitzie said.

> The Lord is my shepherd; I shall not want.
> He makes me to lie down in green pastures.
> He leads me beside quiet waters; he restores my soul.
> He guides me in paths of righteousness for his name's sake.
> Even though I walk through the valley of the shadow of death,
> I will fear no evil, for you are with me.
> Your rod and your staff, they comfort me.
> You prepare a table before me in the presence of my enemies.
> You anoint my head with oil; my cup overflows.
> Surely, goodness and love will follow me all the days of my life,
> And I will dwell in the house of the Lord forever.

Mitzie packed a bag that Mrs. Gracie had made for her, and filled it with cheese, bread and a tiny bottle of water. She scurried under the backyard fence and walked and walked. Mitzie became very tired. She sat down to rest under a fern. "I think I will take a nap," Mitzie said.

Soon Mitzie felt something tug on her ponytail. She jumped up from her sleep and saw the biggest frog she had ever seen before.

"Hey, what do you think you are doing?" Mitzie yelled. She tried to straighten her ponytail.

A deep voice said, "That's a tasty bug; I've never seen anything like it. Can I taste that bug on your head again? It has a sweet tart taste. My name is Bullfrog."

"It's not a bug," Mitzie yelled. "It's a bow Mrs. Gracie gave me." Mitzie started to cry as she thought of Mrs. Gracie. "I was looking for a friend, but I miss my little house and Mrs. Gracie. I want to go home."

"I don't know Mrs. Gracie. Why don't you describe her? I might be able to help you," said Bullfrog. "I travel a lot."

Mitzie rubbed the tears from her face. "Well, she's not too tall for a human, a little belly but not too much. Her hair is brown and gray and combed in a bun. She wears glasses."

"Does Mrs. Gracie have large flowers, fruit trees, fruit bushes, blueberries, and strawberries?" asked Bullfrog.

"Yes, that's her," said Mitzie. "Oh, please, help me get back home."

"What about the friend you are looking for? I do know a little girl mouse," Bullfrog said. "She's about your age, but she doesn't wear bugs on her head."

"That's my bow! I want to go home. Please help me. I'll show you where there are lots of bugs," Mitzie said.

"That sounds like a delicious deal," Bullfrog said.

Mitzie gathered her bag and tried to keep up with Bullfrog who made long leaps into the air. Suddenly Mitzie stopped and yelled. "Help her; help her!"

Bullfrog looked up in the bush where Mitzie was pointing. "Don't worry," Bullfrog said. "Sally Spider is a vegetarian."

"Then why does she have that mouse all spun up?" Mitzie asked.

"She likes to scare everyone to keep them out," said Bullfrog. Bullfrog started to pull away the web with his tongue. Mitzie helped pull with her paws.

"What are you doing here, Bullfrog?" asked Sally Spider.

"Just trying to undo what you have done," Bullfrog said. "Why do you have to go scaring little ones like you do?"

"Because they always mess with my web," Sally Spider said.

Mitzie and Bullfrog finished removing the web from the little mouse. "Mitzie, this is the little mouse I told you about."

"Rainey, stop crying," Bullfrog said. "You need to stay away from Sally Spider. It's the second time she has wrapped you in her web." Bullfrog looked at Mitzie. "Mitzie, this is Rainey. Rainey, Mitzie is looking for a friend." Bullfrog yawned. "Well, I'm all worn out. I need a nap."

"You are always worn out, you old sack of bugs," said Sally Spider.

"You better watch what you say, Sally Spider," Bullfrog said. "I'm hungry and you're starting to look mighty tasty."

"Where do you live?" Mitzie asked Rainey.

"Under toadstools or flower bushes," she said. "I make my own little nest to sleep."

"Would you like to come with me and meet my friend, Mrs. Gracie?" Mitzie asked Rainey. "Mrs. Gracie is very sweet."

"Yes, I would like to meet Mrs. Gracie."

"Just keep going that way and you'll get there," said Bullfrog as he pointed to a fence. "Thank you," Mitzie and Rainey both yelled back to Bullfrog as they scampered away.

Soon they ran under the backyard fence. "That's my home," Mitzie said pointing at her birdhouse. The two mice ran up the tree into Mitzie's home.

"Why do you live in a birdhouse?" Rainey asked. "Where is Mrs. Gracie?"

"It's late; I will explain everything tomorrow," Mitzie said. "We need to say our prayers and go to bed."

"What are prayers?" asked Rainey.

"It's when you thank Jesus for all the things He has given you," said Mitzie.

"Who is Jesus?" asked Rainey.

"The Son of God," Mitzie said.

Rainey watched as Mitzie got on her knees and folded her paws. Rainey did the same. "Thank you, Lord Jesus, for bringing us home safe. Thank you for bringing my new friend home with me. Thank you, Jesus, for Mrs. Gracie. Good night, Jesus."

*In peace, I will both lie down and sleep, For You alone,
O LORD, make me to dwell in safety.*
Psalm 4:8

Mitzie and Rainey

THE FOOD BOXES

Mitzie stretched and yawned. She jumped out of bed and remembered her new friend, Rainey. Mitzie looked over at Rainey sound asleep in her little bed.

She tiptoed out to her porch. Mrs. Gracie had left a food box for her. She smiled and clapped. The beautiful box held all kinds of good things to eat. Mitzie ran back in the house with her box and set it on the table.

She looked over at Rainey still sleeping; Mitzie would save a large part of the food for her.

Mitzie peeked into the box. She squealed softly. "Oh, a grape and cheese and bread crumbs and what's this? I don't think I've ever had this before." She held up something white. "It looks like bread." Mitzie sniffed the white slice in her hand. "But it doesn't smell like bread." She took a tiny bite. "Oh, it's so sweet." Mitzie squealed even louder at the new taste of this delicious treat.

At Mitzie's squeal, Rainey jumped up screaming and hid under the bed. This made Mitzie scream and run under the bed, too. They both huddled close together and shook. Finally, Mitzie turned to Rainey and whispered, "What scared you?"

"I don't know," Rainey whispered back. "I've never been so comfortable in my life. I heard a loud noise and that scared me. Then, you screamed and ran under the bed, too."

"I thought you saw something scary," replied Mitzie. They laughed at each other and rolled from side to side.

"How did you get the name Rainey?" asked Mitzie. "Was it raining when you were born?"

Rainey answered, "No, when I was a baby, I was always crying so they changed my name from Angel to Rainey. My mom said that my tears were as big as rain drops."

"What happened to your family?" Mitzie asked.

"I lost a sister first in a flood, and then I got separated from the rest of my family when we all had to run from a lot of wild cats," said Rainey.

"Maybe you will find your family someday. Mrs. Gracie taught me that if you believe in Jesus anything is possible. She always reads her Bible while sitting under the orange tree. I climb on one of the branches and listen to her read. She puts her finger on the words as she reads, and that's how I learned the words. She gave me a little Bible she had on her keychain. She saved my life when I was a baby."

The back door opened.

"That's Mrs. Gracie. Do you want to see her?" asked Mitzie. "I'm scared of humans." Her big brown eyes filled with tears.

"Mrs. Gracie is coming out to water her yard," Mitzie said.

Rainey peeked out at her. "Oh, she is pretty."

"She gives me lots of food," Mitzie said. "She left a box of food earlier; I saved you some sweet bread crumbs. She left a thimble full of milk, too."

After the two ate, they played together all day long until the sun started to go down.

Mrs. Gracie watched them from the door. "I will have to put more food in the boxes for them. I am glad Mitzie has met a friend."

"Let's go in and have a snack," Mitzie said. "Then I'll read to you from my little Bible." While Rainey finished her snack, Mitzie read John 3:16 to her. "For God so loved the world that he gave his one and only Son, that whoever believes in him shall not perish but have eternal life."

Rainey stared at Mitzie and asked if she could read it again.

Mitzie read it again.

"Mitzie," said Rainey, "could you teach me to read so when I find my family I can teach them to read the Bible?"

"I would be happy to do that," said Mitzie. "Let's go outside before we go to bed."

The two mice looked up at the twinkling stars.

"Look," said Mitzie, "there's a shooting star."

They both squealed and laid flat on their backs to look straight up at the stars. Soon it was time for bed.

"We need to pray every night before we go to bed." They both got down on their knees. Mitzie prayed. "Thank you, Jesus, for Mrs. Gracie and keep her and her family safe. Bless everyone in this beautiful world you created."

"Good night, Jesus," said Rainey.

Mitzie Says Her Prayers

*Rejoice always, pray continually, give thanks
in all circumstances for this is God's will
for you in Christ Jesus.*
1 Thessalonians 5:16-18 (NIV)

Mrs. Candi Spider

Don't Worry

Ms. Candi Spider worked on her web all morning. She stopped when she saw Mitzie and another little mouse.

"Ms. Candi," said Mitzie, "your web looks like Mrs. Gracie's woolen shawls. They only need the bright beautiful colors that Mrs. Gracie uses."

"Thank you, Mitzie," said Ms. Candi. "What are you up to today?"

"I want you to meet Rainey, my new friend," Mitzie said.

"She's really cute. Where did you come from?" asked Candi Spider.

Rainey answered. "From the horse ranch past the big pond."

"I met mean old Sally Spider," said Mitzie. "When I saw Rainey she was all webbed up; I screamed, but Bullfrog told me it was okay because Sally Spider is a vegetarian."

"I thought I was dinner, so I cried a little," said Rainey. "I wouldn't have been afraid if I had known about Mitzie's Jesus."

Mitzie corrected her. "No, he is everyone's Jesus."

"Yes, I see," Candi Spider said. "I hear Mrs. Gracie reading her Bible and praising Jesus all the time when she sits in the backyard under the trees. She thanks him for the orange blossoms when they are in bloom; they smell so good. I have started praising and thanking Jesus too. I hear Mitzie praising the Lord and thanking him."

"If you decide to stay in this area, I will teach you more about Jesus," Mitzie said to Rainey. Suddenly, a giant mosquito dived at Rainey.

Rainey screamed and ran under a toadstool.

Mitzie laughed. "I see you don't like them either. Mrs. Gracie sprays some kind of stuff on herself when she works in her garden. They leave her alone. The big one's name is Skeeter, and he is a real pest. He is worse than the flies."

Skeeter kept flying close to Rainey.

Rainey cried. "I don't want Skeeter to sting me."

"Oh, he's not going to hurt you; he's just a bully," said Mitzie. "Follow me; Mrs. Gracie planted some plants that Skeeter doesn't like."

The two little mice ran under a plant.

"Mrs. Gracie calls this a citronella plant," said Mitzie.

Skeeter saw them and dove down as fast as he could, but he couldn't stop in time. BOOM!

He crashed into the plants. His wings crinkled, his beak bent up, and his eyes spun.

Mitzie and Rainey laughed. Mitzie had never seen him that messed up before. He tried to fly but couldn't because his wings and nose were crooked. Skeeter started walking home.

"Good-bye, Skeeter," Mitzie said. "I hope you feel better soon. We will be here when you want to be friends."

Skeeter looked back at the girls, but his eyes were still spinning. "See you later," he mumbled.

Soon Mitzie and Rainey were off to meet another new friend.

Skeeter the Mosquito

Don't worry about anything.
No matter what happens, tell God about everything.
Ask and pray, and give thanks to him.
Phil 4:6 (NIRV)

MEET EDGER

Mitzie and Rainey ran under the gate to the pond. They climbed to the top of the bricks. "This is so beautiful," Rainey said. "Mitzie, you are so lucky."

"No," said Mitzie. "I am blessed because Jesus loves me, and He loves you too. We need to make Him first in our lives."

"Oh, look—fish—you have fish in the pond." Rainey said.

"Yes," Mitzie answered. "They are called Koi fish."

Rainey stood up to get a better look at the Koi fish. When she turned around, she saw a large gray cat. She screamed. "Cat, Cat, Cat!" She took one step to run away but, instead, she fell into the pond.

Mitzie turned to look behind her. "It's okay; that's Edger; he won't hurt you." Mitzie dropped a fern leaf into the pond so Rainey could climb out on it. "You don't have to be afraid," Mitzie said. "You're all right."

"You weren't the one that fell in the water," Rainey cried.

"Edger, meet Rainey," Mitzie said.

"Hello, Rainey," said Edger. "I'm sorry; I didn't mean to sneak up on you."

"Rainey, this is Edger," said Mitzie. "Edger is a quiet cat. When you get used to him you won't be afraid anymore."

Rainey stopped crying and fixed her wet braids.

"We need to get back home," said Mitzie. "It's getting dark, and I'm starving; aren't you, Rainey?"

"Yes, I am," said Rainey. "What will we eat?"

"Let's go see what Mrs. Gracie left us," answered Mitzie.

"Do you want to hop on my back?" Edger asked, "I'll get you there in a flash."

"Okay," said Mitzie.

"NO," Rainey yelled.

"Come on," said Mitzie, "I'll be right next to you. Aren't you hungry? Mrs. Gracie probably put the food out. If we don't hurry, the ants will get it."

"Okay, but you get on Edger first," said Rainey.

Edger laid down.

Mitzie climbed on his back, and then held a paw out to help Rainey on behind her. "Let's go," said Mitzie.

Edger ran along the side of Mrs. Gracie's house; soon they were at Mitzie's house.

"Look," Mitzie said, "There is a box. No…two boxes."

Mitzie and Rainey jumped off Edger.

"Edger, would you like to eat with us?" asked Mitzie.

"No, thank you," said Edger. "I have other plans. Maybe next time. Good-bye."

The girls waved good-bye to Edger and watched him run off toward the gate.

Mitzie picked up a box, and Rainey picked up the other box. They took the boxes inside, set them on the table, and opened them.

When Rainey opened her box, she asked, "What is this?"

Mitzie answered, "Pizza."

Then Mitzie opened her box.

"What's this?" Rainey asked holding up something from Mitzie's box.

Mitzie answered, "It's pizza with cinnamon and apples on it."

Mitzie and Rainey ate and ate. Soon they were very full.

"Let's leave the rest for tomorrow," said Mitzie. "It's time to clean up and get ready for bed."

After they brushed their teeth, they got on their knees to pray.

Mitzie looked at Rainey. "I am so glad you are my friend, Rainey. We will have so much fun together."

A tear ran down Rainey's face. "I am so glad you found me and taught me about Jesus," said Rainey. "Someday we will find my family, and I will teach them about Jesus."

"Yes you will, Rainey," said Mitzie. Let's pray for them right now. Thank you, Jesus, for giving us plenty to eat. Thank you that Rainey is my friend. Protect Rainey's family. Bless Mrs. Gracie and her family and give them good health."

Rainey finished the prayer. "Thank you, Jesus, for bringing Mitzie and Mrs. Gracie into my life and for them teaching me about You. I will learn Your word so I can teach my family about Your love. Good night, Jesus."

Rainey Meets Edger the Cat

*I have hidden your word in my heart
that I might not sin against God.*
Psalm 119:11

Mrs. Gracie and Mitzie the Mouse

www.ingramcontent.com/pod-product-compliance
Lightning Source LLC
Chambersburg PA
CBHW041220240426
43661CB00012B/1100